Christian CHURCH

Alan Brown and Alison Seaman

Contents

A & C BLACK • LONDON

A Christian church

This book is about a church, a place where Christians go to worship. Christians are followers of Jesus Christ and they try to live their lives according to his example. Christianity began almost 2000 years ago in the country which is now called Israel.

Jesus was called '*Christ*' by his friends and followers. They believed he was their new leader, rather like a king, and so they called him 'Messiah' or '*Christ*'. The word *Christ* means 'anointed' and, even in Britain today oil is poured onto a new king or queen's head to anoint them during their coronation.

This symbol was first used by Christians to represent **Christ**. *It is a sort of abbreviation or shorthand. If you write '***Christ***' in Greek the first two letters are X (chi) and P (rho). Combine these together by writing one on top of the other and it makes the symbol. It is called the Chi-Rho (pronounced ki-ro).*

This painting shows Jesus restoring the sight of a blind man. The **Bible**, *Christianity's holy book, tells how Jesus healed the sick. Jesus' followers were amazed and inspired by his actions and they spread the news about what they had seen to everyone they met.*

There are now Christians in almost every country throughout the world. Wherever Christians have settled, they have built churches as their place of worship.

Churches vary greatly in size and appearance, from plain, small chapels to massive, richly-decorated cathedrals.

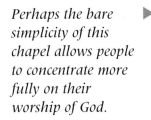

Perhaps the bare simplicity of this chapel allows people to concentrate more fully on their worship of God. ▶

◀ *Some Christians think that church buildings such as this cathedral should be elaborately decorated using the most expensive materials, to celebrate the glory of God.*

Just as churches may look very different to each other, so Christians worship in a variety of ways depending on what type of church they belong to, such as Roman Catholic, Methodist or Church of England. What all churches have in common is that they provide a central place where Christians can meet together to remember and give thanks for the life of Jesus.

The children in this book wanted to find out more about Christianity. They visited their local church, St Mary's at Finchley in London, which is part of the Church of England.

The children were welcomed to St Mary's by the Reverend Joanna Yates, who showed them around the church.

How Christianity began

Most of the *Bible* stories about the life of Jesus describe what happened when he was about thirty years old. It was then that he began to travel around, talking about and teaching about God.

Jesus told stories about everyday life to try to help people to understand his message. Large crowds gathered around him to listen. He became very popular because he was able to heal sick people. But Jesus did not draw attention to his healing work; he was more interested in spending time with the poor and with people such as tax collectors, who were disliked by everyone else.

Although Jesus had many admirers there were also people who were very suspicious of him. His enemies decided he was becoming too popular and too powerful. The *Bible* describes how they wanted to be rid of him and arranged to have him arrested and put to death. Crucifixion was a particularly cruel method of execution. Jesus was nailed to a wooden cross and left to die.

For Christians throughout the whole world, the cross, like the one on which Jesus died, has become the most important symbol of their faith. Churches often contain stained glass windows like this one at St Mary's, which shows the death of Jesus.

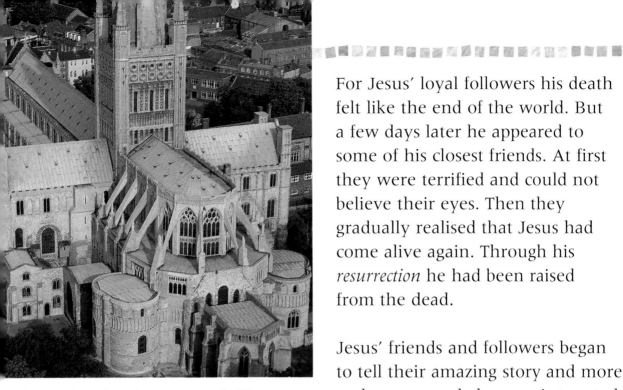

The cross is such an important symbol for Christians that many churches in England are built in the shape of a cross. This photograph of Norwich Cathedral was taken from the air. Can you pick out the shape of a cross?

For Jesus' loyal followers his death felt like the end of the world. But a few days later he appeared to some of his closest friends. At first they were terrified and could not believe their eyes. Then they gradually realised that Jesus had come alive again. Through his *resurrection* he had been raised from the dead.

Jesus' friends and followers began to tell their amazing story and more and more people became interested in hearing about the life of Jesus. Christians today are still spreading the story.

◄

Artists throughout the centuries have tried to find ways to represent the extraordinary events at the end of Jesus' life. This painting of the **resurrection** of Jesus is over 400 years old. Can you describe what is happening in the picture?

What do Christians believe?

Jesus is described in the *Bible* as a wise and effective teacher who was kind and helpful to the people he met, especially if they were sick or disadvantaged.

But, as the Revd. Joanna Yates explained to the children, for Christians, Jesus is far more than this. They believe that God became a human being in Jesus, so they call him the Son of God. Christians believe that through God's *incarnation* as a human being, they are brought closer to God because, through Jesus, he knows what it is like to be human.

Christians also believe they can feel God's strength and power in their own lives through the spirit of God. They often refer to God in three ways: God the Father; God the Son, Jesus Christ; and God the *Holy Spirit*. The one name that includes all these three is the *Trinity*. This way of describing God is a central and most important Christian belief.

The children found different sorts of crosses in the church. Joanna explained to them that a crucifix shows Jesus' body nailed to the cross. A plain empty cross reminds Christians that Jesus rose from the dead.

This child noticed the symbol of a fish on a hassock, a special cushion on which Christians can kneel when they pray. Each letter in the Greek word for fish stands for the initial letters in the Greek phrase 'Jesus Christ God's Son Saviour'. Why do you think there are three fishes in the picture?

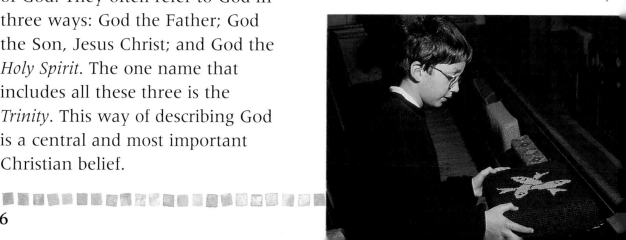

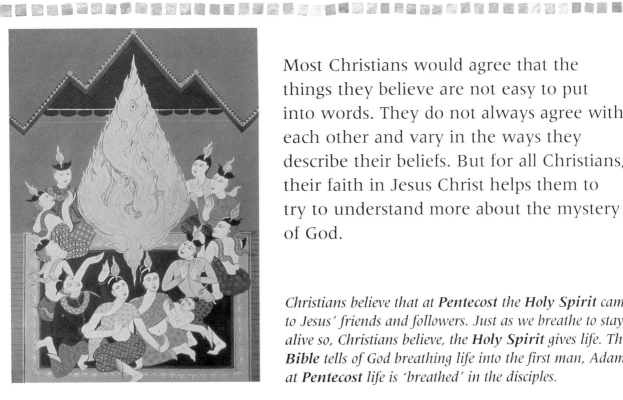

Most Christians would agree that the things they believe are not easy to put into words. They do not always agree with each other and vary in the ways they describe their beliefs. But for all Christians, their faith in Jesus Christ helps them to try to understand more about the mystery of God.

*Christians believe that at **Pentecost** the **Holy Spirit** came to Jesus' friends and followers. Just as we breathe to stay alive so, Christians believe, the **Holy Spirit** gives life. The **Bible** tells of God breathing life into the first man, Adam; at **Pentecost** life is 'breathed' in the disciples.*

*The **Holy Spirit** is often represented as in this painting, as a rushing wind. In the language of the **Bible** 'spirit' can mean 'breath' or 'wind', even 'life'. The dove in the picture is a symbol of peace. Christians believe that Jesus is their hope of everlasting peace for the world.*

The Bible

The *Bible* is a sacred book for Christians. Sometimes it is described as the Holy Bible because it is a book about God. Although it looks like one book, it is really a collection of many books, that can be dipped into rather than read one after another.

There are two main parts to the *Bible*, the Old Testament and the New Testament. The books of the Old Testament were first written in Hebrew, and tell the story of the Jewish people. These are the scriptures Jesus knew and on which he based his teaching.

*The first **Bibles** were written by hand and were often beautifully illustrated. This one is over 500 years old. Can you imagine how long it must have taken to make? Look carefully at the picture. Can you recognise an event that Christians celebrate every year at Christmas?*

The books of the New Testament were first written in Greek in the hundred years or so after Jesus' life on earth. They tell about events in the life of Jesus and about the first Christians. The first four books in the New Testament are called the *Gospels* and are named after the people who are thought to have written them: Matthew, Mark, Luke, and John.

*In Joanna's **church** there is a large copy of the **Bible** that can be seen by everyone. It is kept on a high stand called a **lectern** which is in the shape of an eagle. The eagle is a powerful bird that flies high in the sky and it is also the symbol of Saint John, one of the **Gospel** writers. The children could see how the outstretched wings of the eagle provided a firm resting place for this very special book.*

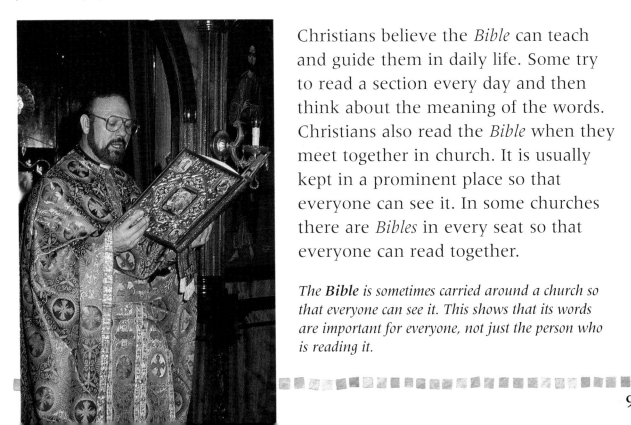

Christians believe the *Bible* can teach and guide them in daily life. Some try to read a section every day and then think about the meaning of the words. Christians also read the *Bible* when they meet together in church. It is usually kept in a prominent place so that everyone can see it. In some churches there are *Bibles* in every seat so that everyone can read together.

*The **Bible** is sometimes carried around a church so that everyone can see it. This shows that its words are important for everyone, not just the person who is reading it.*

How do Christians worship?

When Christians worship they are not just remembering God the Father, God the Son and God the *Holy Spirit*. They are honouring and praising something which they feel is far greater and more important than themselves and their everyday lives.

Christians believe they can talk to God and listen to God anywhere and at any time but they also find it helpful to pray together. Looking around St Mary's, the children felt that the church was a very quiet and peaceful place and that the atmosphere would help people to feel closer to God.

The very first Christians were not able to build churches and so they met for worship in each others' homes. Some Christians still prefer to do this today.

Christians meet and worship together in a variety of places from huge cathedrals to open fields. What matters to Christians is simply being together and worshipping together. In this way a church is a group of people not just a building.

Christians like to feel close to God in different ways. In some churches, people light candles when they say a prayer. The light is a symbol of hope that God will hear their prayer. ▶

The most important day for Christians to worship together is Sunday, because it marks the day on which Jesus rose from the dead. It is such a special day, that Christians consider Sunday to be the first day of the week.

When Christians meet together in church, their worship often follows a routine called a service. There will be hymns and prayers and *Bible* readings, which change from day to day. Different churches follow different patterns of worship, but a service usually includes singing, talking, praying and silence.

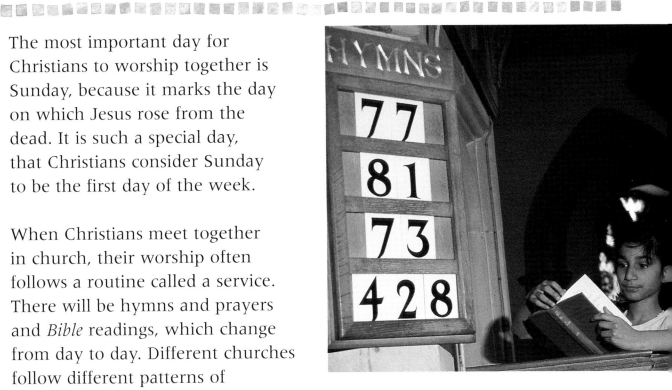

*During church services hymns are often sung. Poonam looked at the numbers on the **hymn** board which told her where to find the hymns in the **hymn** book. There is usually an organ or piano in the church to accompany the singing.*

People of all ages worship together. There is usually something in the service for everyone. Children often have special roles: carrying candles, helping the *priest*, or being a member of the choir.

◀

In this church the choir are leading the singing. Music plays a very important part in the worship.

At the front of St Mary's, the children came to the large table called the *altar*. During a service a special meal of bread and wine is prepared by the *priest* at the *altar* and then served to everyone in the congregation who wants to take part. This sacred meal is known by various names; Holy Communion, *Eucharist* (which means thanksgiving), Lord's Supper, or Mass. To understand why this meal is so important to Christians, you need to find out more about Jesus' life .

Just before Jesus was arrested and killed, he met with his closest friends and they shared a meal. Many Christians believe this would have been the Jewish Passover meal. The *Bible* describes how at this meal Jesus shared around the bread and wine to his friends. He then asked them to do this every time they met together and, as they ate the bread and drank the wine, to remember him.

*The **altar** at St Mary's is covered with beautiful, richly embroidered cloths. It is often decorated with flowers, candles and a cross or **crucifix**.*

◄

When Jesus met with his friends on the night of his arrest, he shared bread and wine with them. This meal, the Last Supper, has become a very important part of Christian worship.

When Christians share this special meal of bread and wine they are remembering what Jesus asked of his friends: 'Do this in memory of me'. It is a way of re-enacting that last meal that Jesus shared with his friends just before his death. Christians feel they come very close to God when they share bread and wine together.

*Joanna showed the children how she prepares the sacred meal of bread and wine. In her church a thin wafer of bread is used. The wafers are kept on a silver plate called a **paten**. Everyone has a small sip of wine from the same silver cup called a **chalice**.*

What does a priest do?

Some Christians choose to devote their lives to working for the Church. They are known by various titles, such as *priest*, vicar, minister or pastor. They are leaders and teachers in their community just as Jesus led and taught his followers. You can often recognise a *priest* or a minister because of the special collar (sometimes called a dog collar) worn in their shirt.

Joanna is one of the *priests* in her church and she showed the children some of the special clothes she wears when she leads the worship. The clothes might be plain and simple or very brightly coloured and elaborate; they are often decorated with Christian symbols.

When Joanna lays out her *vestments* she makes the scarf and the belt into the shape of an alpha and an omega, the first and last letters of the Greek alphabet. In the *Bible* these are used to describe God as being the beginning and the end of everything.

*This long white robe Joanna wears is called an **alb**. She also wears a long scarf around her neck and a rope belt around her waist.*

*The beautiful red silk robe, which she puts on last, is called a **chasuble**.*

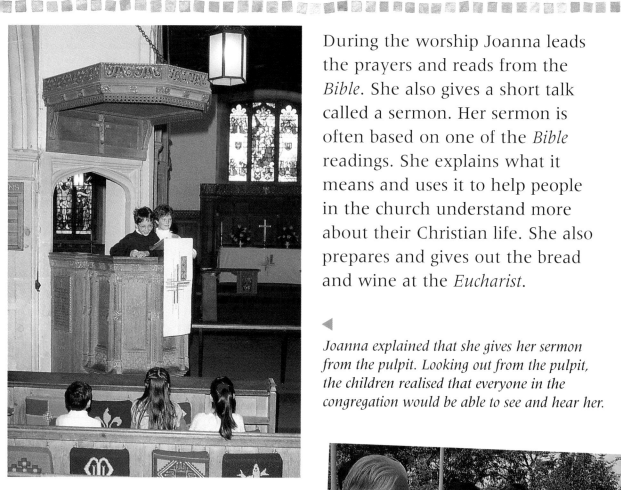

During the worship Joanna leads the prayers and reads from the *Bible*. She also gives a short talk called a sermon. Her sermon is often based on one of the *Bible* readings. She explains what it means and uses it to help people in the church understand more about their Christian life. She also prepares and gives out the bread and wine at the *Eucharist*.

◄

Joanna explained that she gives her sermon from the pulpit. Looking out from the pulpit, the children realised that everyone in the congregation would be able to see and hear her.

As well as spending time looking after the church, Joanna also works in the local community. She goes to see the elderly in her parish and people who are ill, and she is a regular visitor in her local primary school. Joanna spends a lot of her time in meetings organising church events and making sure the parish runs smoothly. She often meets with people from other churches and people of different faiths.

▲

*Before the bread and wine are served, they are blessed by the **priest**. During the prayer they are offered to God and made holy. For many Christians it is as though Jesus is there with them at the communion meal.*

The Christian year

Christians all around the world remember events in the life of Jesus by a regular pattern of festivals, which are celebrated in church as well as at home.

In many churches the Sunday worship is planned on a calendar with chosen themes for each week, such as *Advent* Sunday, Mothering Sunday, and Whit Sunday. There are *Bible* readings and prayers which relate to the chosen theme.

The children went outside the church to look at the bell tower. In the past, before everyone wore a watch, people would rely on the church bell to find out the time of day and to remind them when it was time to come to worship. On festival days or for special celebrations such as a wedding, the bells would ring out in long peals.

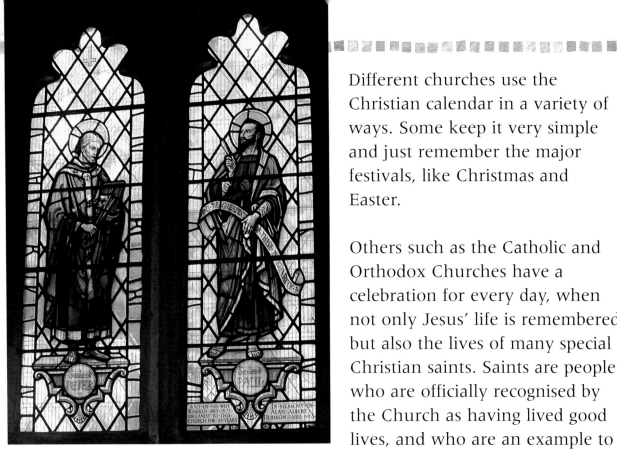

All around St Mary's the children found stained glass windows showing pictures of famous Christian saints, such as St Peter and St Paul. You can read about the lives of these saints in the New Testament.

Different churches use the Christian calendar in a variety of ways. Some keep it very simple and just remember the major festivals, like Christmas and Easter.

Others such as the Catholic and Orthodox Churches have a celebration for every day, when not only Jesus' life is remembered but also the lives of many special Christian saints. Saints are people who are officially recognised by the Church as having lived good lives, and who are an example to other Christians.

The children discovered that in churches like St Mary's, colours are used to decorate the church at certain times of the year. The *priests* will also wear matching colours at these times. For example, red is used to celebrate *Pentecost* and white is worn at Christmas and Easter.

Jesus' mother, Mary, is a very important figure for many Christians around the world, because they believe that she is the mother of God. Churches often contain statues of Mary, or beautiful pictures of her, called icons. Services in these churches celebrate festivals associated with Mary's life.

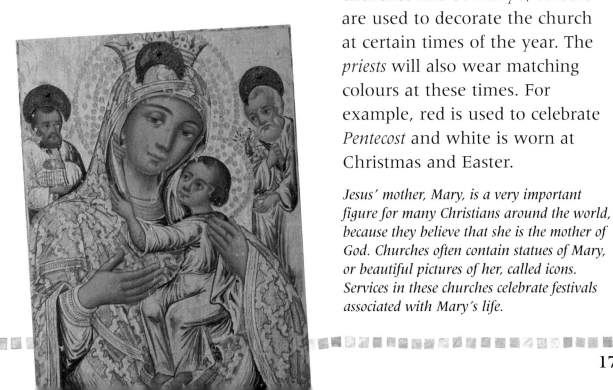

Lent and Easter

The most important Christian festival is Easter when Christians celebrate the new life they believe Jesus offers to them. During *Lent*, the weeks before Easter, Christians prepare for this special time. They will often meet together to study the *Bible* and to talk about their Christian lives and responsibilities. In the past, *Lent* was a time when Christians would fast. Some Christians still try to go without certain foods or something they normally enjoy.

▲

*When Jesus was committed to death he was forced to walk through the streets carrying the cross on which he was to be crucified. The **Bible** describes how he suffered and fell to the ground many times. These events are remembered by Christians on Good Friday, the most solemn and sad day in the Christian year.*

◀ *On each Good Friday, in Jerusalem, Christians carry a cross through the streets to the hill called Calvary where Jesus was crucified.*

Many churches also look solemn and bare during *Lent*. All the colourful decorations and flowers are removed. It is a way of reminding Christians about the time Jesus spent alone and without food, thinking about what might happen to him in the future.

The last days of Jesus' life are commemorated during Holy Week. Christians remember these by reading the *Bible*, by acting the events of the stories or by thinking and praying about the terrible suffering and death of Jesus.

*On Good Friday the **altar** at St Mary's Church is stripped bare.*

*In contrast, on Easter Day the **altar** is beautifully decorated once again. The Easter candle is lit to remind Christians that Jesus rose from the dead.*

But Christians believe this was not the end of the story. On Easter Day, they celebrate Jesus coming back to life. Churches are once again full of colourful decorations and flowers. It is a time of great hope and joy. Some Easter services start off with the church in total darkness and end with it flooded with light with everyone holding candles as a reminder of Jesus' new life.

Advent and Christmas

For Christians, Easter is the most important festival, but for most people Christmas is the best known. Almost every church will celebrate the birth of Jesus because this is the time when Christians believe God came into the world. It is such a special time that it needs to be prepared for, carefully.

In the Church's year, *Advent* means 'before the coming' and it is the time when Christians prepare themselves for this very special gift from God, the gift of Jesus.

Christians light candles as a reminder that Jesus represents the light of God coming into the world. A candle is lit on each of the four Sundays in *Advent* as Christians prepare for Jesus' birth. A fifth candle is lit on Christmas Day to represent Jesus' arrival in the world.

The children looked at the crib in St Mary's Church. The model is used to illustrate the story of the birth of Jesus every Christmas. It shows the baby Jesus in a stable with Mary and Joseph looking on. ▷

The Christmas story is illustrated in one of the stained glass windows at St Mary's. The children were discovering how every part of the church building could tell them something more about Christianity.

Children in some churches today make christingles as part of their Christmas celebrations. An orange is used to represent God's world. Four sticks are pushed into it to represent the four corners of the earth and on each of the sticks are sweets to symbolise the fruits of the earth. In the top of the orange is a candle to represent Jesus. A red ribbon around the orange reminds Christians that Jesus died for them.

The Christmas festival lasts for twelve days. The story of the birth of Jesus is often acted out in the church, there are candlelit services and carols and *hymns* are sung. Even church members who do not come to church regularly, join in the atmosphere of peace and forgiveness.

The festival ends with *Epiphany*. The Christmas story in Matthew's Gospel describes how wise men came to visit Jesus and bring him precious gifts. *Epiphany* means the 'showing' of Jesus and in many churches, the wise men are put into the crib scene, bringing their gifts to the baby Jesus. Jesus is 'shown' to them and Christmastide is over.

The Church family

The life of the church is the life of its people. Just as we mark special times in our own lives, like birthdays and anniversaries, so the church marks important times in the lives of its members.

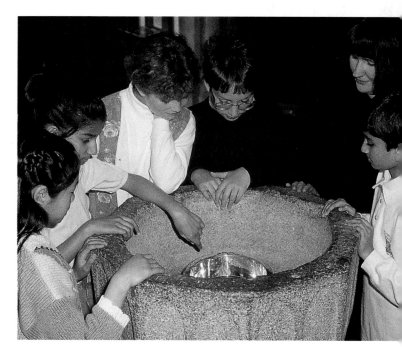

*Joanna showed the children how she prepares for a **baptism**. This large, old stone container is called a font. It is where Joanna puts the water to pour over the baby's head.*

The *Bible* tells of Jesus' baptism, in the River Jordan, when he was a young man. Babies are brought to church to be baptised. *Baptism* is a way of joining God's family and the whole church. The word '*baptism*' means 'immersion' and so water is poured over the baby's head. The family are given a candle as a symbol of hope for the child's new life.

Some Christians believe that it is better to baptise people when they are adults and can decide for themselves whether or not they wish to be baptised. These Christians hold the ceremony in the sea and are completely immersed in the water.

When couples get married in church they make their promises before God and in the presence of their family and friends. Their happiness is shared by everyone.

At sad times, too, the church family will get together to pray and to give comfort to each other. This may be when a person dies, and at the funeral thanks are given to God for their life. Christians believe that after death they will be with God; death may be the end of their earthly life but it is the beginning of a new life, closer to God.

Inside the church, the children found memorials to members of the church who had died.

In the graveyard outside the church the children found the tombstones which marked the graves of people who had died. The stones gave the names of the people who were buried there and the date of their death.

Behind the scenes

When Christians meet together in church, they can get to know each other better and offer help and support to each other. Churches live by people's energy and enthusiasm. Members meet not only to share their faith, but also to work together to try to make the world a better place.

Young people's groups, *Bible* study groups and play groups for babies and young children often take place in the church or in rooms nearby. Many churches have 'drop-in' times when anybody can visit the church and meet with other people for a chat over tea and biscuits.

When you hear some good news the first thing ▲ you want to do is tell everyone about it. Christians believe that the events in the life of Jesus are so important that they are like good news. Christians spread the 'good news' in many different ways.

The children looked at the notice board in St Mary's to find out about the events that happen in the church throughout the week, ▼ as well as on Sunday.

At harvest time gifts are distributed by the children to elderly people living near the church. Churches often have a list of members who go out into the community and visit the elderly or the sick. People who are not able to leave their homes can become very lonely, so they look forward to seeing a friendly face.

St Mary's regularly produces a church magazine with news about what is happening in the parish. People who attend St Mary's read the magazine but it is also useful for people who are, for example, not well enough to come to church, but like to know about the events taking place there.

The congregation at St Mary's want it to be a warm and welcoming place where anyone can feel safe and at home. It is important to them that the church always looks its best. Each week members of the church come in to arrange flowers, sweep the floors and polish the woodwork. Many churches have cleaning rotas and flower rotas so the responsibility is shared between different people.

Many people in the parish give up their free time to make sure that St Mary's always looks its best.

Christians believe that God created the world and that they share in the responsibility of caring for God's world. They are committed to trying to make the world a better place in which all people can live together. This means that Christians try to speak out against the things they think are unfair and wrong. They try to follow the example of Jesus by helping those who are poor or homeless, or who do not have enough food to eat.

Desmond Tutu was Archbishop of Johannesburg in South Africa. He has always spoken out against injustice and argued that all people, whatever their race, colour or religion should be treated equally.

Probably one of the best known Christian organisations is the Salvation Army. You may have heard one of their bands playing carols around the streets at Christmas. Their real work is caring for people who need help, particularly the lonely and the homeless.

Working with people who are homeless is a major part of the work of the Salvation Army. Having someone there to listen can make all the difference for people who feel lonely and unwanted.

Churches often hold fund raising activities to raise money to help people in need. The money may be used in the local community, or it may be sent to a Christian organisation which helps people in different parts of the world. Perhaps your school has helped to raise money to support the work of Christian Aid or CAFOD or Pax Christi?

In this Christian Aid 'Projet Integre de Podor' local people are taught how motors, engines and pumps work. Sharing knowledge and skills is one of the ways people can help each other to work together for a better world.

Time-line

These important dates in the history of Christianity are shown as BCE (before the common era) and CE (meaning 'in the common era'). This dating system can be used by people of all faiths. The use of BC 'before Christ' and AD 'Anno Domini – in the year of our Lord' is based on Christian beliefs.

6 BCE – 30 CE
Jesus is born, probably around 6 BCE. He dies about 30 CE.

40 – 65 CE
Paul becomes a follower of Jesus and writes a number of letters to growing churches.

MARY AND JESUS

1560 CE
The Reformed Church is established in Scotland.

1500 – 1700 CE in Britain
This is the time when the Church of England is created. Henry VIII breaks from the Church in Rome and becomes head of the Church of England.

Most of the present building of the church of St. Mary's at Finchley dates from the 1600's.

1500 + CE
The invention of the printing press makes Bibles more widely available. New churches are set up and people are encouraged to think more for themselves about their beliefs.

1611 CE
The King James version of the Bible known as the Authorised Version is first published.

HOLY BIBLE

1662 CE
The Book of Common Prayer is published for use in all Church of England churches. It is still used in some Anglican churches today.

1700 – 1900 CE
Other religious groups such as Methodists and Congregationalists are founded.

Missionaries take Christianity to every corner of the earth during this period.

1865 CE
The Salvation Army is founded.

60 – 100 CE

During this period the four gospels were written. Followers of Jesus became known as Christians and are persecuted.

100 – 200 CE

Persecutions increase and continue for another century. Christianity spreads across Europe.

200 – 500 CE

Christianity is brought to Britain by people like Ninian and Columba. Their sort of Christianity is called 'Celtic Christianity'. It is strongest in Ireland, Scotland and North.

500 – 700 CE

Augustine is sent from Rome to Southern England to teach Christianity. He founds a school in Canterbury in 597 – the first church school in England.

ST FRANCIS

700 – 1000 CE

Roman Christianity spreads rapidly in Britain. Parish churches are built – often of wood.

There has been a church on the site of St Mary's at Finchley from this time.

1500 – 1700 CE

A period of change in Europe. During the Reformation, Martin Luther from Germany and John Calvin in Switzerland encourage people to break from Roman Catholicism. They, and their successors, are called 'Protestants'. Each group persecutes the other.

1200 – 1500 CE

The monks of St Francis of Assisi and St Dominic spread through Europe teaching and preaching.

1000 – 1200 CE

Some of the old and great abbeys and cathedrals are built. Monks become a part of British religious life.

1900 – 2000 CE

Two world wars help different Christian groups to come together. There is a growing understanding between many Christians.

1942 CE

British Council of Churches is founded. In 1990 it became The Council of Churches for Britain and Ireland.

1948 CE

World Council of Churches is founded.

OIKOUMENE

How to find out more

Visiting a church

You may be able to make the initial contact with your local church through a parent or 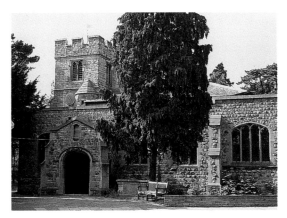 colleague at school. The first approach can be made by telephone but should be followed by written confirmation outlining the arrangements and the purpose of your visit.

Your host in the church will find it helpful to know the age of your pupils and any preparatory work they have completed. A preliminary visit is always advisable, to familiarise yourself with the surroundings. You will be able to prepare a frame-work for the children's activities once you have decided on the focus of your visit e.g. Christian symbols, worship, the building, the people.

It is unlikely that you will be visiting the church during a service but, as a place of prayer and worship, the pupils will be expected to behave quietly and respectfully. There are no specific dress codes required when visiting a church but modest dress is always considered appropriate for any religious building.

Your host will inform you of the parts of the building where the pupils can roam freely and those areas that are out of bounds.

Christian artefacts

Throughout this book there are examples of artefacts used in St Mary's Church. Your local religious communities may be prepared to loan artefacts to you. You could also make your own collection. Christians from different denominations use artefacts in a variety of ways, and a collection of religious objects can help to illustrate the diversity of practice.

The following artefacts would be appropriate for your collection:
cross, crucifix, palm cross
chalice
paten
candles eg baptism candle, confirmation candle, Easter or Paschal candle, memorial candle
a collection of greetings cards eg Christmas, Easter, baptism, first communion, confirmation/church member-ship, ordination prayer cards
Bible, Prayer Book, service books, orders of service eg baptism, marriage, funeral
rosary beads
icon

Useful words

Advent The period at the beginning of the Christian year. It begins on the fourth Sunday before Christmas. The word advent means *coming*.

alb A garment worn by a priest. It is a simple white tunic reaching to the ankles.

altar The table, used for the *Eucharist*, on which the bread and wine are prepared.

baptism A ceremony to mark entry into the Christian family. This can take place either as a child or as an adult.

Bible The Christian holy book. It is a collection of smaller books grouped into two sections described, by Christians, as the Old Testament and the New Testament

chalice A goblet or bowl used to hold the wine served during the *Eucharist*. It could be made of pottery or a more precious material like silver or gold.

chasuble A semi-circular garment worn by a priest over the *alb*. A different colour of chasuble is worn at different times in the year.

Christ Meaning *the anointed one* and the name given to Jesus by his followers.

church The religious building used by Christians for worship. The word church is also used to describe a group of Christians and sometimes to describe Christians all over the world.

Crucifix A cross with the body of Jesus hanging on it.

Epiphany The festival, twelve days after Christmas, which celebrates the coming of the Magi (Wise Men) to the baby Jesus.

Eucharist A word meaning *thanksgiving*. A service in which the death and resurrection of Jesus are remembered in a meal of bread and wine.

Evangelist A writer of one of the New Testament's four Gospels. The word is also used to describe someone who preaches the Gospel.

Gospel An account of the life and work of Jesus. In the New Testament there are four Gospels written by Matthew, Mark, Luke and John.

Holy Spirit The third part of the Trinity. Christians believe God is alive, active and present in the world through the power of the Holy Spirit.

hymn Songs of praise about events in the life of Jesus and about life as a Christian.

incarnation The Christian belief that God came into the world as Jesus of Nazareth.

lectern A stand on which the *Bible* is displayed in church.

Lent The 40 days leading up to Easter.

paten The plate on which bread is prepared and served during the Eucharist.

Pentecost Also known as Whitsun (White Sunday). The festival which commemorates the coming of the Holy Spirit to the followers of Jesus 40 days after Jesus' ascension into Heaven.

prayer A way of communicating with God.

Priest A spiritual leader within the Christian community.

Resurrection The rising from the dead of Jesus Christ.

Trinity The Christian belief in God as three persons in one; Father, Son and Holy Spirit.

vestments The special clothes worn by a *priest* during a church service.

Index

First published 1997
A & C Black (Publishers) Ltd
35 Bedford Row
London WC1R 4JH

ISBN 0-7136-4337-4

© 1997 A & C Black (Publishers) Ltd

A CIP catalogue record for this book is available from the British Library

Acknowledgements
The authors and publishers would like to thank the Revd. Joanna Yates and Asif, David, Emily, Mei Yee and Poonam for their generous help in the preparation of this book.

All photographs by Jak Kilby except for: pp 2, 5b, 8, 13a, The Bridgeman Art Library; p3a Historic Scotland; p3b ZEFA; p5a Skyscan; p7b St Paul Multimedia; p7a The Asian Christian Art Association; pp 9b, 10b, 11b, 21b, 27a David Rose; pp10a, 15b, 17b, 18b, 22b, 24a, 25a, TRIP Photographic Library; p18a McCrimmonds; p23a Newport Photographic; p26a Popperfoto; p27b Christian Aid

All artwork by Vanessa Card

Produced in the E.C. by *Partenaires-Livres*® on SCA paper